19.85   3-14-02   Southeastern   T

LET'S GO! LET'S PUBLISH!
Katharine Graham and the Washington Post

Makers of the Media

LET'S GO! LET'S PUBLISH!
Katharine Graham and the Washington Post

Nancy Whitelaw

Greensboro

LET'S GO! LET'S PUBLISH!: *Katharine Graham and the Washington Post*

Copyright © 1999 by Nancy Whitelaw

Photo Credits:
AP/Wide World Photos

Library of Congress Cataloging-in-Publication Data
Whitelaw, Nancy
  Let's go! let's publish : Katharine Graham and the Washington post
/ Nancy Whitelaw. —1st ed.
      p. cm. — (Makers of the media)
  Includes bibliographical references and index.
  ISBN 1-883846-37-4
      1. Graham, Katharine, 1917- Juvenile literature. 2. Publishers and publishing—
United States—Biography—Juvenile literature. 3. Washington post (Washington, D.C. :
1974)—History—Juvenile literature. 4. Newspaper publishing—Washington (D.C.)—
History—20th century—Juvenile literature. I. Title II. Series.
Z473 . G7W48 1999
070 . 5' 092—dc21
[B]

                                                                    98-46284
                                                                       CIP

Printed in the United States of America
First Edition

Dedicated with love to Evelyn Diers, a woman of great courage.

Contents

Katharine Graham

Chapter One

___

"I was the peasant walking around brilliant people"

In 1972, Katharine Graham, chief executive officer of *The Washington Post*, faced the most difficult question in journalism. Who should define the public's right to know? When did the government have the right to refuse permission to publish?

At issue were the Pentagon Papers, a government-sponsored top secret study of the history of the Vietnam conflict. The *New York Times*, scooping *The Post*, had printed excerpts from the papers. The government objected, saying that military security was threatened by publication. The federal courts issued a restraining order on further publication of the papers by *The Times*, pending an investigation.

Early the next morning, Katharine had possession of the papers. She was under no restraining order because officials did not know she had them. If she moved quickly, *The Post* might print at least some of the papers before they too were restrained.

She had two options. She could publish, opening herself to government charges of treason. Or she could withhold publication, opening herself to journalists' charges of violating the public's right to know.

She described making her decision: "Frightened and tense, I took a big gulp and said, 'Go ahead, go ahead, go ahead. Let's go. Let's publish.'"

* * *

Katharine "Kay" Rhoades Graham, who has been called "the most powerful woman in America," suffered from shyness and an inferiority complex from early childhood in the 1920s right into her adult life. When she was older, she wondered about the roots of her insecurity. She thought of one possible reason: "I came from this incredibly high-powered family." As a child, she said, "I thought I was the peasant walking around brilliant people."

Her father, Eugene Meyer, was a multi-millionaire known throughout the country for his work with charities. Her mother, Agnes, was a member of high society in both Washington, D.C. and New York. Her oldest sister, Florence, was in Kay's words, "beautiful in the classic sense." Her next oldest sister, Bis "Elizabeth," was daring, flamboyant, often in the limelight. Next came Bill who needed no badge of superiority beyond being male, a fact which gave his mother "a ridiculous sense of achievement."

Next came Kay, in 1917—not beautiful, not flamboyant, not a male. Three-year-old Kay lost her only claim to fame—that of baby in the family—in 1921 when Ruth was born.

Kay worried about not being smart. Her father's firm, Eugene Meyer and Company, had opened the first research department on Wall Street. Her mother studied art, the Chinese language and Eastern religions. Her sisters and brothers, from two to seven years older than she was, were ahead of her in everything—learning to ride a bike, swimming, reading, having close friends, riding horseback.

She worried about not being socially acceptable. Her parents had guests for dinner almost every night—people high in social, political, and financial circles—but Kay was not allowed to eat with them until she was nine years old. She couldn't go on family summer camping trips either, until she reached that somehow magic age of nine. Her older sisters and brother saw her as a nuisance, such a tattletale that they once taped her mouth shut.

During and after World War I, Kay's childhood centered in

Eugene Meyer made his fortune on Wall Street before he decided to purchase a newspaper.

Washington, where her father worked for the government at volunteer jobs (one dollar a year payment) on the War Industries Board, the War Savings Committee, and for the War Finance Corporation. Her mother attended a steady round of dinners, teas, parties, charity organizations, and clubs. She visited with some of the famous people in the world—statesman Bernard Baruch, physicist Albert Einstein, sculptor Auguste Rodin, photographer Edward Steichen, painter Georgia O'Keeffe.

The children saw very little of these busy parents. Once Bis suggested: "We ought to have a blackboard at our front door like the one at school where notices are posted. Then when we go out, we could see whether you are going to be home when we come back from school it would help a lot."

Eugene and Agnes usually ate breakfast by themselves, but occasionally they invited the children to talk with them at that time. Sometimes Agnes let one of the children visit with her while she got dressed. Eugene was not often home for dinner, but when he was, he arranged impromptu debates with the children. Agnes described these dinners: "my husband would constitute himself chairman of the meeting and call upon each child, regardless of age, to rise and state his case." Eugene was quick to point out what he considered to be faulty reasoning.

When the parents were not available, the children spent time with the dozens of servants who took care of the children, cooked, cleaned, chauffeured, and gardened in the two family homes. With servants everywhere, Kay became used to being waited on from the moment she woke up in the morning until she got ready for bed at night. She was scarcely aware that she lived in a grand and extravagant style. She knew that she would be a wealthy adult because her father had set up trusts for each of the children, to be opened when each turned twenty-one. Until then, each child received an allowance and could not spend beyond that.

One of their Washington homes was a large house called Crescent Place, a mansion with stately columns and a fountain in the front yard. The children used the coach house as a play house. The large back yard became a playground for neighborhood children.

The family spent much of the summer at Mt. Kisco, New York, in a mansion which overlooked a lake where they could boat and fish. With pigs, chickens, cows, orchards, and gardens and seven hundred acres, Mt. Kisco was somewhat like a farm. It was also an entertainment center with an indoor swimming pool, a bowling alley, a tennis court, two dining rooms, and many large paintings and sculptures.

But summer days were not lazy days when Eugene and Agnes were around. Kay's schedule began at breakfast when she gave a report to her father on her progress in both academics and athletics. Sometimes Eugene gave her a little quiz on her summer studies. He praised her highly when she did well. Agnes, too, showed concern about her children's achievements. But she used criticism instead of compliments to pressure her children to succeed. When ten-year-old Kay proudly told her mother that she had read all of *The Three Musketeers* by Alexandre Dumas and Auguste Maquet, Agnes was not impressed . She said that she had read that book in the original French when she was Kay's age. Still, Kay loved reading. She read all the Louisa May Alcott books, *Treasure Island* by Robert Louis Stevenson, and many adventure books.

From nine o'clock until noon, they had lessons in math, history, literature, and French. In the afternoon, they had lessons in swimming, riding, dance, French, and tennis. Dancing lessons brought particular discomfort to Kay who simply could not relax. "I hated it," she said. Her French teacher would often scold her, calling her a scatterbrain. The scolding made Kay more nervous, not more careful.

Both parents emphasized competition. They set an example by playing an endless game of dominoes. Week after week, month after month, they kept score, with the winner bragging to the children.

This home schedule prepared Kay nicely for her classes at Potomac Hill Elementary School. She knew how to be attentive and how to follow a schedule. But the social situation at the school presented some problems for her because she had not learned to get along well with her sisters and brother. She finally figured out a way to cope, and that was to model herself after her classmates who were successful both in classes and in popularity. Fifth grade was a good year for Kay. Her dancing and acrobatics classes gave her strength and agility. She was pretty good at races, volleyball, and other sports. A teacher pointed out to her that she might become captain of a team if she weren't so bossy. Kay took her advice and became captain.

When Kay was nine years old, she could finally go on the summer family camping trips. Her mother called these trips "hair-raising" and "perilous." She claimed that these trips helped the children to become independent and to look after themselves. However, to be on the safe side, she took along five ranch hands and seventeen pack horses on each trip.

Agnes also took the children on archaeological trips. The expeditions were well planned to include servants and archaeologists as well as the children. They explored in New Mexico, California, and the Canadian Rockies.

When Kay was considered old enough to eat with guests, she learned that mealtimes were more than opportunities to chat with the family. The Meyer lunch and dinner tables often included twenty or more people, invited for their opinions, prestige, or influence. The guest lists usually included people of political status like Supreme Court justices, senators, and presidential candidates as well as those well-known in arts, music and letters.

When she was in the eighth grade, Kay went to dancing school where she was humiliated for several reasons. First, she was one of the tallest in the class. Second, her mother had suddenly decided to cut down on spending so Kay had to wear her sisters' hand-me-down

Kay's mother Agnes often communicated with her daughter by letter.

dresses. To make things even worse, she had to wear gold kid shoes with two-inch heels since they were the only style to fit her fast-growing feet.

On the fun side, Kay and her friends traded samples of soap and shampoo and photographs of favorite movie stars like Greta Garbo and Marlene Dietrich. They read a lot of movie magazines. Kay had dreams of becoming a model or of being famous for some reason she had not figured out yet.

Maybe she just wanted to be well-known because her parents were. One of Agnes' prestigious projects was creation of a summer camp for underprivileged children. In 1924, she was a delegate to the Republican National Convention that nominated Calvin Coolidge for president. Eugene served as commissioner of the Federal Farm Loan Board under President Coolidge.

Kay went to high school at Madeira, an all-girls college-preparatory school in the center of Washington. The studies were rigorous—language, economics, science, philosophy, and general college preparation courses.

The 1930s were the era of the Great Depression when unemployment created hunger, poor housing, and lack of medical care for millions of United States citizens. Miss Madeira, the head of Kay's school, challenged her wealthy students to become aware of these social problems. Every year, the girls held a Poverty Party and donated the proceeds to a social welfare fund. Another aspect of Miss Madeira's philosophy involved public service. Through a school connection, Kay was an assistant in a hospital in ninth and tenth grade.

Most of the students boarded at the school on weekdays under strict supervision from Miss Madeira. No girl could go shopping without a chaperone; no student could visit in another student's home if only the father would be there. But Kay and her friends managed a little unsupervised freedom. They took part in a secret society that occasionally met in the middle of the night in the woods.

Dances were held twice a year at school. No boys were allowed. The girls wore evening dresses and flowers, and they danced with each other. Since Kay was so tall, she was often the leader in the dancing couple.

Kay did very well at Madeira in all phases—academically, athletically, and socially. She was class president, head of the student body, and editor of the school paper *The Tatler*. She played varsity basketball, hockey, and track. She took piano lessons and appeared in a school play. Although she believed she had little self-confidence, her class prophecy predicted that she would be a success in the newspaper business.

In the spring of 1933, Kay heard her mother and father talking about Eugene's recent purchase of *The Washington Post*. When she expressed surprise, her mother said, "Oh, darling, didn't anyone tell you? Dad has bought *The Post*."

Chapter Two

"I had a certain lack of direction"

The Washington Post, first published in 1877, was called a Democratic daily by the owner, Stilson Hutchins. The first editions were four pages long, cost three cents, openly supported the Democratic Party, and had a circulation of about ten thousand. In 1889, Hutchins sold the paper for $175,000 to the partnership of Frank Hatton and Beriah Wilkins. The partners announced the goal of the paper: "The Post will have very decided opinions on all public and other questions." The business was incorporated as The Washington Post Company. That year, the daily paper ran from twelve to fourteen pages, and the Sunday editions, thirty to thirty-six pages. The price was still three cents for a daily and five cents for Sunday.

In 1905, would-be politician John McLean bought *The Post* from Hatton's and Wilkins' heirs. One of his goals for the paper was "to print always the good about the city-both in the news and editorial departments." In 1911, the price of the daily paper was lowered to two cents, and circulation rose from twenty thousand to thirty thousand. In 1914, the Sunday edition of the paper featured four pages of color comics and seventy-four pages of editorial at a cost of five cents .

In 1916, Ned McLean inherited *The Post* from his father. By 1921, the paper, floundering under stiff competition from other Washington papers, tried to attract readers with stunts-a contest for prettiest feet, a marathon, life insurance for new subscribers, cooking lessons. The paper built its audience with readers who were interested in such stunts and in the light news and features offered by the paper. In 1924, Ned McLean was involved in the Teapot Dome financial scandal, which resulted in the imprisonment of the secretary of interior. McLean was not jailed, but the public lost faith in both him and the paper. McLean's business policies grew more lax, and he suffered from alcoholism. In 1929, the family refused Eugene Meyer's offer of five million dollars for the paper.

In 1932, the depth of the Great Depression, *The Post's* circulation fell to about 50,000. Many advertisers withdrew their support. In 1933, the paper defaulted on bills for newsprint, and the courts took over the company. At a public auction, Eugene Meyer beat out two other potential buyers with his bid of $825,000 for the paper.

Eugene had finally fulfilled a long-held dream. Now he hoped to stay in public life, using the paper to make his views known to Congress and other political groups. On June 13, 1933, Meyer announced on the front page: "It will be my aim and purpose steadily to improve *The Post* and to make it an even better paper than it has been in the past."

Eugene had bought lots of problems. The paper was housed in a forty-year-old building. The broken-down presses were held together with wires. Circulation had dropped to the lowest of the five Washington papers. Many of the best writers and managers had already left the paper, sensing imminent sale or bankruptcy. And the head of the rival *Herald* persuaded the comics syndicate to stop selling comics to *The Post*. Suddenly, it lost the faithful readers who had looked forward to "Dick Tracy," "Gasoline Alley," "Andy Gump," and "Winnie Winkle."

Eugene went to work to increase circulation. He created a strong new women's section. He started a popular advice column. He enticed good employees by offering them high wages. He started a lawsuit against the syndicate to get the comics back. He strengthened the editorial page with forceful opinions backed up by facts.

During the summer after she graduated from high school, Kay worked at *The Post* as a copy girl/ messenger. She worked just for something to do, not from any idea of becoming a journalist. In fact, she had no long-term goals, and this frustrated her. It seemed to her that everyone else had exciting personal and professional goals. Flo enjoyed a glamorous social life, Bis studied in Munich, Germany, for a year, and Bill studied at the London School of Economics. Kay knew only that she wanted to go to Vassar, an all-girls college in Poughkeepsie, New York. Even this was not an exciting decision. She chose Vassar only because both her sister and Miss Madeira had gone there.

Her goal for herself that summer of 1934 was to become popular with boys. After studying the popular girls, she thought up a plan. Part of the plan was to laugh as loudly as she could. Another part was to pretend that she was always having a great time. She also began to take an interest in what she wore. She found endless fault with the clothes that her mother bought for her: "too short under the arms," "too short-waisted." "I looked like the original scarecrow in it."

In her first year at Vassar, Kay had to learn a lot that was not in the curriculum. She had always had servants to take care of her clothes, meals, and other personal responsibilities. At college, no one picked up her dirty clothes, prepared the foods she liked, or cleaned her room. The other girls laughed at her because she wore the same yellow sweater until she went home for Thanksgiving, never giving a thought to the fact that it had to be washed. Accustomed to having her time scheduled by teachers and parents, she didn't know how to set up a study schedule for herself. In her history class, she did so poorly that she was put on probation. She received no sympathy at home. No matter what books she mentioned, her mother said she had already read them and knew all about them.

President Franklin Roosevelt's attempts to help the poor and unemployed encouraged many of Kay's generation to become politically active.

Kay read *The Post* every day. She frequently wrote to her parents, discussing what she read in the paper, showing special liking for stories with a human interest angle. Her studies in economics and history helped her to understand the articles, and her conversations with fellow students helped her to form opinions about the editorials.

Kay found herself among young women who were eager to become activists. Many of the professors supported President Franklin Delano Roosevelt. The students often debated the policies of this Democratic president who created hundreds of government-sponsored programs to help the unemployed and poverty-stricken. They held endless arguments about the extent to which the government should spend tax money to help individuals and companies. Among the causes they worked for were financial help for the poor, jobs for the unemployed, and government aid to farms and factories.

She became interested in the ever-present conflicts between labor and management. Although she had never held a job, she readily supported the thousands of workers who declared that they were underpaid, overworked, and often placed in dangerous work situations. Carrying the argument further, she said that students were also workers and, therefore, they had a responsibility to help their brothers and sisters in jobs to fight for better work conditions.

As military conflicts grew in Europe throughout the thirties and threatened to erupt in a world war, a group at Vassar loudly opposed United States involvement in the conflicts. Students demonstrated on the main streets of Poughkeepsie in favor of peace. Talk increased about German leader Adolph Hitler's persecution of Jews. Kay did not feel any personal involvement in this persecution; she had never thought of herself as Jewish. She knew that her father was Jewish and her mother Lutheran, but the children did not become involved in religious activities. Her Jewish background became significant when one of her friends mentioned that she would never have a Jewish guest in her house. Kay was astounded.

Kay made her debut at home with a dancing party in December 1935. Most debutantes wore white for their coming-out; Kay wore a gold dress with large shoulders and puffy sleeves.

She was tall and pretty with black curly hair. In new groups, she was somewhat shy, but became outgoing in a group in which she felt comfortable. Like her peers, she dressed for classes in worn-out dirty saddle shoes, tweed skirts, and sweaters. She was elected to Daisy Chain, a group of sophomores judged to be the prettiest students in the class and so chosen to take part in the graduation ceremonies.

Kay assumed some leadership responsibilities. She founded the Liberal Club, and was elected an officer in the Political Club. She represented Vassar at the founding convention of the American Student Union. This group was particularly controversial because most of its members were communists, socialists, liberals, and radicals—all intent on reforming American economy and politics.

Letters from her mother were always written by Agnes' secretary. Each letter began with "Your mother says ...." The letters Agnes dictated to her secretary focused on what she was doing and whom she was meeting. They told of her mother's fascination with Thomas Mann, author of *The Magic Mountain* and other novels, and with other men known in social and cultural circles. Agnes described a thrilling interview with Mann she did for *The Post*. She wrote to Kay: "Be a newspaperwoman, Kay, if only for the excuse it gives you to seek out at once the object of any sudden passion."

Communication with her father centered on his work at the paper. In 1935, he admitted that the paper had lost more than $1.3 million. He also admitted that circulation figures were low, and *The Post* had a poor reputation as a news source. But he added, he was fascinated with the challenges ahead of him

Before the end of her sophomore year, Kay felt dissatisfied with the curriculum and the challenges at Vassar. She suggested to her father that she attend the London School of Economics to study economics, as Bill had done. Her father refused; he was worried about the growing military tension in Europe. But he agreed that it was time for her to leave Vassar. He suggested the University of Chicago which had just inaugurated the Chicago Plan, a new program with a focus on ideas, primary sources, and the classics. Kay agreed. She liked the idea of the Chicago Plan, and she looked forward to living in a city. Also, the school was known as a radical one, partly because of its innovative idea that women could and should receive the same education as men. Kay welcomed a move farther away from her parents. It would give her a more distinct feeling of being on her own.

She knew that she could stay in close touch emotionally with her father through letters and phone calls. Her mother, never close anyway, was increasingly involved with her projects and more interested in politics and educational reform than in her children.

In the summer of 1936, Kay went to Europe with a friend. There she became more involved in workers' struggles. In France, she took part in a march supporting workers there. As for her own career, Kay said, "I could picture myself working but not in any high-up position. I think it was typical, no women thought they could do anything."

In September 1936, Kay was in Chicago, alone in a strange environment with only a couple of casual acquaintances. She promised herself to give it a try, and she also promised that she would return to Vassar if this new adventure didn't work out.

She met students of much greater diversity than at Vassar. Many students from lower middle-class families attended; many of these worked their way through school. She roomed at International House where she made friends and acquaintances with students from all walks of life. Most of the residents at International House lived on one of the eight floors, sharing a single bathroom with others on that floor. Kay had her own private bathroom. Despite her wealth, her clothes reflected the typical U. of C. student—sweaters with skirts below her knees, ankle socks, and saddle shoes.

Often, she picked up the tab when she and her friends went to Hanley's, the local tavern, for ten-cent-a-glass beers. When friends wanted a ride, she drove them in a big black Buick, which her brother had given to her. She was a little embarrassed about bringing friends home with her between semesters. She feared that they would see the elegant living style as a crude ostentatious display of wealth.

Besides many required courses for her major in American history, Kay took a course in the great books of the Western world. These classes were seminars which met only once a week. Assignments included heavy reading and thoughtful preparation for class. In the seminars, students were asked to form and defend their opinions on philosophical problems like: What are good habits? Does good behavior follow from good habits? What does Aristotle think about this? Kay performed very well in these seminars, continually improving her ability to write and to state her opinions. Perhaps her father's dinner table debates gave her a big advantage.

She found her classes stimulating, made wonderful friends, and generally enjoyed her life. She still was searching the "who-am-I" questions that had always plagued her, but felt more directed in her life nevertheless. Again, the subject of her Jewishness came up. A friend said she would try to have Kay tapped for membership in a sorority even though she was Jewish. Again, Kay was surprised, and she decided not to try to join the club even if they would consider her. She frequently dated Sidney Hyman, publisher of a radical magazine. There she again ran into anti-Semitism. She discovered that many of her fellow students believed that dating a Jew—Hyman was a Jew—could hinder a girl socially.

As at Vassar, Kay continued her sympathy toward the labor movement. She joined the Chicago branch of the American Student Union. The ASU leaders were strongly aware of her father's position and prestige. They assigned her to the executive committee, openly in hopes of using her influence, money, and political connections.

One of the group activities was a drive for clothing and food for Spanish soldiers fighting against against the army of the facist leader, General Francisco Franco.

During a strike at Republic Steel in south Chicago, Kay accompanied a journalist friend who was covering the action. She saw strikers fired on by police. She gave out pamphlets urging the closing of sweatshops where workers spent long hours in unhealthy conditions for little pay. She passed out coffee and offerred to babysit striker's children while they demonstrated.

Some ASU members tried to persuade Kay to join a student group supporting communism. She was tempted because of her sympathy with workers. On the other hand, she embraced capitalism, realizing that her parents would never have succeeded so well financially under a communist economy. She could not support the overthrow of a system that had given her all she had.

She kept up her interest in journalism by carefully reading *The Post* each day and sometimes writing criticisms of articles to her father. One of her letters expressed disgust at the policy of *The Post* concerning President Roosevelt. Kay insisted that the newspaper was inconsistent to welcome Roosevelt after his election because they had written many editorials opposing his candidacy. Her father did not agree with her. He said that Kay was forgetting the function of journalism, which was to help people to understand and appreciate the democratic process.

Her father wrote that he was pleased with the growing success of *The Post*. Circulation doubled to 112,000. Advertising had also doubled. He brought well-known writers to the paper—columnists Walter Lippmann and Dorothy Thompson—as well as popular comics, daily crossword puzzles, and other reader-pleasing copy. He spent time getting to know local politicians and other leaders so that he would be in line for a scoop whenever one of them wanted publicity. He wrote Kay that she should get right down to *The Post*

Eugene Meyer hired Dorothy Thompson to write a column for the *Washington Post*.

as it was growing fast: "You ought to be in on the job of putting it [*The Post*] to the top."

Agnes faced increasingly serious personal problems, emotional outbursts and bouts with depression. Kay knew that her mother was drinking heavily. Kay worried about her younger sister, Ruthie, who was still in high school at Madeira. She tried to take some responsibility for her younger sister, paying more attention to her whenever she could.

Kay also grew closer to Bis. Her older sister, still glamorous, worked in California and numbered among her friends Queen Marie of Romania, musician George Gershwin, and author Dorothy Parker. Despite the difference in life styles, Kay and Bis shared some good conversations. Bis understood when Kay admitted that she had problems because the rest of the Meyer family was so successful. She wrote Kay a letter telling her that she understood, and she said that all the Meyer children felt the same way. Kay answered, comparing the Meyer family ties to "an octopus, whose tentacles stretch far and wide and, what is worst of all, deep." She told Bis that she wanted to become a journalist specializing in labor reporting. But they both knew, she said, that her father wanted her to work on the business side of *The Post*.

Neither of her parents attended Kay's graduation in 1938 when she received a Bachelor of Arts in history. Her mother sent a note of congratulations, but it was written by a secretary who spelled Kay's first name incorrectly. She refused her father's offer to return to Washington to work on *The Post*. She didn't want to live near her parents, and she wanted the satisfaction of getting a job on her own. Still, she was undecided about her future. "I think I knew what I wanted," she said, "but I didn't know how to go about getting it. I had a certain lack of direction."

Chapter Three

"I thought he was so great"

At the suggestion of her economics professor, Kay got a job at the *Chicago Times*. But shortly after she began work, she went on a trip to San Francisco with her father. She fell in love with that city, and she asked her father to help her get a job there.

The *San Francisco News* agreed to hire her for two months. That sounded good until she actually went into the office to work. Suddenly, she was hit with the fact that she didn't know anyone in the office, could not type well, and knew nothing about the city. She told her father that she had changed her mind and would be happy to work with him in Washington. Eugene told her not to give up so soon. Perhaps he was speaking in both their interests. He wanted Kay to succeed for herself, and he also wanted her to broaden her experience in journalism so that she would be even more valuable to *The Post* when she got to Washington. He convinced her to stay, and after a month, she loved her work and life in California.

At first, much of her work was simply writing and re-writing articles from phoned-in reports. Kay used some of her first week's salary of $21 to join the Newspaper Guild. She proved herself in her first position and was asked to do some feature assignments. Then the labor reporter on the *News* assigned her to help him with a story about a strike. Part of this assignment included getting to know the longshoremen in the International Longshoremen and Warehousemen's Union. One part of the task was to report on railroad cars filled with strike-breakers, to record what happened as each car stopped at a warehouse to leave the replacement workers.

She also spent hours at the Pacific Coast Labor Bureau. The manager there said she was ". . . a very objective reporter, a digger . . . She certainly wasn't shy when she wanted to find out about a story." The editor was surprised and thrilled: ". . . Miss Meyer showed a remarkable grasp of the issues and events. Soon she was our chief outside reporter on the strike."

After her labor assignments were finished, she took on a number of feature stories, including a suicide, a homicide, and a sex murder. An especially exciting assignment was covering the opening of the Golden Gate Bridge.

Her father asked her to send him copies of her stories. She sent, as well, information on her social life—drinking with union leaders, going to dinners at elegant restaurants, attending the opera. He advised her not to spend so much time in leisure activities. He also told her that *The Post* was still not doing well in competition with two other Washington newspapers. Try as he might, he could not match the circulation of the *Times-Herald* nor the advertising power of the *Star*. He asked his daughter to come back to Washington to help raise *The Post* from its third-place position and to work on decreasing the heavy annual deficit.

Kay didn't want to go back to Washington. As she wrote to her older sister, "What I am most interested in is labor reporting . . . He (Dad) wants and needs someone who is willing to go through the whole mile, from reporting to circulation management, to editorial writing, and eventually to be his assistant."

But like *The Post*, the *News* was not doing well financially. Kay realized that she could lose her job at any time. So when her father appeared in San Francisco to try again to persuade her to come back to Washington, Kay agreed. She accepted a job at twenty-five dollars a week. Introducing his daughter to readers of *The Post*, Eugene wrote, "If it doesn't work, we'll get rid of her."

Her first duties included choosing and editing letters to the editor, writing headlines, laying out the opinion page where readers expressed their ideas, and writing editorials on minor topics.

Her next assignments included writing features and editorials on diverse subjects like folk songs, women and defense work, and popular baseball star Lou Gehrig. She also sat in on editorial conferences and worked in both the advertising and circulation departments. She helped with assembling pages, learning how to place stories for the appropriate impact.

Kay loved the glamour of Washington, the politics, the seemingly unlimited career possibilities for bright and dedicated young people. Her acquaintances at *The Post* soon led her to a full social life with other young journalists, government workers and well-known people like Supreme Court Judge Felix Frankfurter, writer Archibald MacLeish, and corporate lawyer Francis Biddle.

At a party, Kay met Phil Graham, clerk to Justice Frankfurter. Phil was handsome and had received some of the highest grades ever recorded at Harvard Law School. On their first date, Phil told Kay that they would marry. They had many interests in common—friends, politics, writing and editing, enthusiasm about their careers and futures.

On the third date, Phil proposed. "I was really startled," Kay said, "because I thought he was so great." Kay suggested that they ought to wait at least a month before marrying. Phil agreed. But Kay didn't really need a month. She believed she had found the man of her dreams. He had intellectual, physical, and social appeal. She loved him, and he loved her.

Kay invited Phil home to dinner, curious about how Phil and her father would get along. She needn't have worried. Phil and Eugene were soon happily discussing and arguing about racial prejudice, politics, and other matters. After Phil left, Eugene said he very much enjoyed talking with him. Agnes also liked him.

The prospective in-laws did not have much in common. Phil's father was a widower running for re-election to the Florida senate. Ernie "Cap" Graham strongly opposed President Roosevelt and believed that Phil had been too easily influenced by Roosevelt supporters in Washington. Cap did not try to hide his anti-Semitism. The young couple did not let the Grahams influence their decision. They even talked about moving to Florida where Phil might enter political life as his father had.

One concern about the future did arise in Kay's mind. Phil lost self-control and became very drunk on a date. Kay had seen what alcohol did to her mother, and she was determined to talk to Phil about his drinking when he recovered. But somehow she let the matter slide on their next date, and after that it seemed too late to mention it.

Phil also had a concern about the marriage, and he aired it fully before the ceremony. He asked her to agree to live on the income that he could earn himself and not to accept any money from her family. The only exception would be if Kay wanted to make a large donation to charity or some other good cause. Kay had no concerns about accepting money from her family for any reason, but she submitted to Phil's request out of concern for his pride.

Less than six months after they met, Kay and Phil were married at the Mt. Kisco home by a Lutheran minister. Kay wore a long silk off-white gown designed by Bergdorf Goodman. The short guest list included only Kay's family and a few close friends. Phil's father did not attend. He had resisted the idea of Phil marrying a Jew from the first time he met Kay. Phil decided that it would be best if he were not invited to the ceremony and if he and Kay visited his family afterwards as man and wife.

After a honeymoon in Bermuda, Kay and Phil went to Florida. Cap Graham welcomed Kay to the family. Kay experienced no anti-

Kay married Phil Graham, shown here addressing a newspaper trade group, on June 5, 1940.

Semitism in the Graham home, but she was shaken to see a sign in an apartment house that said "No dogs or Jews allowed."

Back in Washington, Kay suggested that they get along without a maid. She made very little working for *The Post*. It would be more economical for her to do a maid's work than to continue with the newspaper. Phil refused: "I don't think I could stand having you wait around with a pie for me to come home from the Court."

So Kay continued with her writing, expanding into articles about social events and also writing some book reviews. Then she was promoted to writing for a column titled "Outlook" where she received assignments for stories with strong human interest, including one about union vs. management conflicts, one on the use of propaganda in America, and another on the conservative America First Committee. She was recommended for and joined the Women's National Press Club.

Phil continued his work as clerk for Justice Felix Frankfurter. Many evenings he would invite several other clerks to their home to continue arguing about cases. Frankfurter became a personal friend to both Phil and Kay.

The war in Europe raged on. Kay agreed with President Roosevelt's view that America should help the Allies—England, France, and other countries—in their fight against the Axis—Germany, Italy, Spain. *The Post* was one of the first major American newspapers to encourage American involvement in the war in Europe. Phil sent many memos to the president, encouraging him to gear up for war.

As the war in Europe widened, Eugene invited two families of his French relatives to come to America to escape the holocaust, the systematic persecution of Jews by Hitler and his Nazi soldiers. Because of this family focus on persecution of Jews, Kay became even more aware of her own Jewish background. As she read about Jewish persecution in Europe, she became more aware of Jewish persecution in the United States.

Eugene continued to struggle to get *The Post* on a sound financial basis. Two papers—the *Times-Herald* and the *Star*—remained top competitors. Despite its shaky finances, *The Post* earned praise for editorial excellence. Writer Felix Morley brought to the paper its first Pulitzer Prize, one of several awards given annually for outstanding achievement. *Time* magazine called the paper "... a journal of national importance, a reading must on Capitol Hill ..." Circulation was up over 170 percent in 1941, but the paper was still losing three-hundred thousand dollars a year. The problem seemed to be that Washington was not big enough for two morning newspapers, *The Post* and the *Times-Herald*.

Kay suffered a miscarriage in late 1941. When she became pregnant again, she determined to relax and give her body a rest. She cut down on her writing and formal entertaining schedule. For several months, she spent time visiting friends, going out for lunch, and doing simple housework chores.

On December 7, 1941, the Japanese attacked Pearl Harbor, Hawaii, and the United States declared war on Japan. *The Post* was scooped in the announcement by the *Times-Herald*, but the headlines were the same in both papers: "U.S. At War."

Immediately, Phil tried to enlist. He was rejected for two reasons: his poor vision and his status as a married man. He became an attorney for the Office of Lend Lease, working to secure loans to defense plants and other suppliers of war materiel. Then he moved into other agencies involved in defense work just as Eugene had done during the First World War. He built a firm reputation as a man who could get things done.

Despite this success, Phil still wanted to join the military. He asked Justice Frankfurter to help him. Frankfurter wrote a letter of recommendation for him, praising his "zeal, intrepidity, complete devotion to the task at hand . . . and the sparkling humor that makes the wheels go 'round."

Kay hoped that he would be rejected again. Their first child was still-born, and she was devastated. But enlistment rules had eased, and Phil was accepted in the Air Corps. As a college graduate, he could have accepted a commission as an officer, but he turned it down because he hoped to see more action as an enlisted man. In a letter to Kay, he wrote that in the two years since their wedding, he had becoming increasingly aware of how important she was to him and how much their marriage meant to him.

In July 1942, Private Phil Graham was sent to Atlantic City for basic training. When he was shipped to a communications school in South Dakota, Kay went to live with him in the military camp of forty-five thousand people. Kay enrolled in a typing and shorthand course to help pass away the long days while Phil was on duty.

The future of the paper was uppermost in Eugene's mind, and he kept Phil and Kay informed through letters. He was creating what he wanted to become a family institution. Of all Eugene's children and their spouses, only Phil seemed a likely candidate to follow him in the management of *The Post*. (He did not consider Kay a potential owner because she was female.) Eugene discussed his hopes with Kay. He bragged that *Post* editorials had earned a fine reputation for logic and presentation. Both circulation and advertising had increased. She reported to Phil: "You better watch out if you don't want it is all I can say. You may find it in your stocking Christmas morning." Phil answered that he still held his long-standing desire to do public service, perhaps through politics. Although he felt positive about the editorial excellence of the paper, he worried about a business relationship with his father-in-law.

Phil did some more thinking about becoming an officer. He was told that he could probably stay in the country and teach if he earned a commission. This sounded good, especially in view of Kay's problem pregnancies. In January 1943, he entered Officers' Candidate School in New Haven, Connecticut, and Kay returned to Washington to wait for him. Before Phil left, he and Eugene had more talks about the future of *The Post*. Phil continued to balance Eugene's offer with his once-stated desire to work in politics.

In May, Second Lieutenant Phil Graham was ordered to a camp in Washington state to teach combat training. Kay was too pregnant to leave with him. She enjoyed quiet times with her father, and they both rejoiced that *The Post* broke even for the first time in 1942. She even took a part-time job for Eugene, reading and critiquing other newspapers for ideas.

In July, after a worry-filled pregnancy, Kay gave birth to Elizabeth Morris Graham. By a lucky coincidence, Phil was back in Washington when she was born. Kay's father came too, but her mother did not show up. At first, Kay thought she would take care of the child, soon nicknamed "Lally," by herself. She soon changed her mind and hired a full-time nurse.

Phil went to Air Intelligence School in Pennsylvania. After six months there, he accepted a position as instructor in the school. For the first time in months, Phil and Kay were living together at least semi-permanently. This created a burden on Kay since Phil was often sick, sometimes from over-drinking, sometimes from something they vaguely defined as the flu. When both Phil and their maid, Mattie, were ill, Kay had to learn how to cook and keep house. Her inexperience led to frustration and tears.

Although he had expected to stay in the country, Phil was sent to the Pacific in the summer of 1944, where he worked in intelligence. Phil's letters to Kay were full of praise for the work of the enlisted men and for the relationship of the officers with these men. His letters to Eugene discussed the good and bad of the issues of *The Post* that he received. With these critiques, Phil was doing from the Philippines what Kay had done from Vassar many years before.

Pregnant again, Kay took a job at *The Post* to keep her mind off her problems. She answered complaints in the circulation department. She did not think of taking on a management position because she "was honestly convinced that women were inferior to men."

Phil came home for a short leave in April. Together they chose a house and talked about how to get it prepared for them before the baby came. When they went to the real estate agent to make the final plans, he told them that area was zoned against sale to Negroes and Jews. They could not buy the house. Kay was shocked. Phil said he didn't like the house anyway.

Kay was left to buy another house on her own. Again she realized what a sheltered life she had led. She had no idea of mortgages or financing. After she managed to get through the paper work, she had no ideas about decorating or how much to spend.

In April 1945, Donald "Donny" Edward Graham was born close to Phil's thirtieth birthday.

Less than a month later, the war in Europe ended. Then, in August the war in the Pacific ended. In September, Phil learned that he would be home soon. Now he had to make a big decision about his career.

Chapter Four

"I was put on earth to take care of Phil "

Phil's father urged him to enter politics in Florida. His father-in-law urged him to work for *The Post*. Kay carefully did not try to sway him. This would be his career and his decision.

On January 1, 1946, Phil joined *The Post* as associate publisher. The couple moved back to Washington. Phil took responsibility for the editorial page, the newsroom, and the city desk. He was aware of his weak background in publishing so he worked hard, intent on learning everything he could as fast as he could.

He also created and maintained communication with some of the most important people in Washington. A mutual relationship was important here. The paper could influence publicity for certain projects and concepts; the people involved could make sure that *The Post* heard about the latest developments first.

Kay retired from all her newspaper duties. One reason was that the men who had left their jobs at *The Post* returned to this country as civilians ready to be hired again. Another reason was that she thought she might like to be home with the children for a while.

Some of Kay's friends remarked that she was more timid, more obedient to Phil than before he went away. One friend commented that Phil was like Agnes, "bright, sharp, [and] could charm the birds off the trees, he was potentially cruel ...self-centered, self-important, arrogant ..." And like Agnes, Phil did not hesitate to criticize Kay.

Whatever the relationship changes, Kay became more and more involved with the children and housekeeping. She struggled, working at relating to the children, to Phil, and to the housekeeping responsibilities. The relationship with Phil proved the most difficult. Phil was over-working and over-socializing to the point where they were seldom home alone together. They became a part of Washington social life, socializing with the most important people in town from government circles. "I saw myself as being the adjunct to Phil's life," Kay said.

To friends and co-workers, Phil seemed happy with his family and his job. But Kay knew different. She lived with his alternating periods of optimism and pessimism. Phil described his moods: "Yesterday I was saturated with gloom ...Today for no good reason I feel quite jubilant ..." Such mood swings were familiar to Kay, who had seen her mother a victim of this form of depression.

Agnes wrote for *The Post* on a wide variety of topics including segregation, poor schools, political corruption, and problems of migrant workers. These articles were well-researched and interesting, but they usually exceeded the expected word limit. She created a reputation at *The Post* for her strong objections to any changes in the manuscripts she submitted. At one point, Agnes was so enraged over being edited that she wrote to Phil that she would never again have anything to do with the paper or any of its employees. Phil took the necessary time to calm her down and change her mind. When Agnes drank too much at home, Eugene escaped to his office.

In the winter of 1945-46, *The Post* became involved in a controversial international issue. Citizens in war-torn Greece, Italy, Yugoslavia, and Poland were starving. The United Nations prepared to send aid, but Congress refused to vote funds to help support this project. Furthermore, the secretary of agriculture declared that America did not have the surplus wheat predicted, so the United States would not send millions of tons of wheat abroad as promised.

When President Truman asked Eugene Meyer to help run the new World Bank,
Phil Graham assumed control of the *Washington Post*.

Eugene reacted angrily in an editorial. On March 10, a notice appeared in *The Post*: "This is a time for greatness. It is not a time for vengeance. . . . If America does not feed the hungry, the hungry will die." With this statement, *The Post* created a Famine Emergency Committee. The goal of the committee was to cut down food waste in America to produce a surplus to send overseas.

In the spring of 1946, President Truman asked seventy-year-old Eugene to head the new World Bank. Eugene told Phil and Kay that he didn't want to be president of the World Bank. All he wanted to do was to run the paper and through the paper to fight for what he thought was right. Still, he believed it was his public duty to answer the call of the president. Phil encouraged him to take the job. Eugene took the job and suddenly thirty-year-old Phil became publisher of *The Washington Post* after only five months on the staff. He was the youngest publisher of a major paper in American history. Eugene put an announcement in the paper on June 18: "I am withdrawing from the active direction of its (*The Post's*) affairs and shall have no control or responsibility over news or editorial matters."

Phil accepted these duties at a time when *The Post* still suffered from competition against other papers. The *Star* made more money and the *Times-Herald* had better editorial quality and more advertising volume. Phil went right to work on a plan to increase coverage of European events. To further this goal, he attended the peace conference in Europe and hired the first foreign correspondent for the paper.

Kay believed that they needed a grander home now that Phil was publisher. She found an eight-bedroom house that she loved near Georgetown, one with a suite for the children including their own dining room and playroom. They put in an offer of $115,000, lower than the suggested selling price of $125,000. When Eugene learned of this, he paid the difference, and the couple bought the house for them. Kay accepted, breaking her earlier promise to Phil not to take money from her parents. Kay enjoyed decorating it in velvet and mahogany with lots of paintings.

Only a week after Eugene took up the new position, he realized that the board of directors of the World Bank was not interested in his ideas and expertise. In December 1946, less than six months after he accepted the job, he quit. Back at the paper, he took the position as chairman of the board while Phil retained the title of publisher. He did not criticize the many changes that had been made while he was gone. He let Phil know that he would be available at all times to study situations and to offer suggestions. But as time went on, he expected more consultation than Phil gave him. Tensions between the two men grew. Kay tried to encourage Phil to be more gentle with her father.

Kay became involved in welfare work, fund drives for the Community Chest and the National Symphony. She was on the board of directors for a children's convalescent home. She was also very busy with their children, assuming most of the responsibility for their education and leisure time. She described her attitude: "I really felt I was put on earth to take care of Phil Graham. He was so glamorous that I was perfectly happy just to clean up after him." Although the couple did a lot of entertaining, the choice of social activities was almost always left to Phil.

After just one year on the paper, Phil was definitely in charge and knowledgeable—and ready to take risks. He analyzed every aspect of the paper, from editorials to sales to suburban coverage to mechanical problems. He searched out and described problems, set new objectives, and made plans to follow through. He was an extremely effective advertisement salesman. From the beginning, he was involved in labor negotiations. In 1947, *The Post* won the National Headliners' Club award for outstanding public service. The Newspaper Guild said about the paper: "It (*The Post*) is a vivid demonstration of what an outstanding newspaper is like and what it can do in serving its readers, its community and the country."

In the spring of 1948, The Washington Post Company bought a majority share of CBS Radio in Washington. That year the paper reached new highs in both circulation and advertising. It employed 800 workers, enjoyed a circulation of 180,000 daily, and won a number of prizes for writing and for public service. Eugene was satisfied that Phil would continue the tradition of the paper as Eugene had established it. He transferred the voting stock of the paper to Phil and Kay, and he created a trust with a board of five people who would have control if Phil and Kay left the paper. In his press release, he said that he was confident that under Phil and Kay the paper would maintain its principles of independence and public service.

Eugene gave Phil $75,000. He gave the same amount to each of Kay's siblings. With this money, Phil bought five thousand voting shares in the firm. Most of the shares were in his name. Phil explained why he had more voting shares: "A man should never feel that he is working for his wife." If Phil died before Kay, she would become the majority stockholder, with the rest of the shares going to the four Graham children. Kay dismissed all thoughts that she would eventually control the paper: "[Phil] thinks I'm an idiot. Honestly, I have no influence."

In September 1948 after the birth of William Welsh Graham, their third child, Phil asked Kay to write for "The Magazine Rack," a Sunday column of that reviewed current periodicals. Kay accepted the job because she believed that she needed a new interest in her life. Her column became one of the most popular in the paper, and she enjoyed the challenge.

When the owner of the *Times-Herald* died in July 1949, Phil immediately put in a bid to buy the paper. His $4.5 million offer was matched by one from Colonel Robert McCormick, owner of the *Chicago Tribune*. When she learned this, Kay urged Phil to increase his bid, and he did so. But the McCormick proposal was accepted, partly because the deal would help to solve an estate problem. *The*

Post's major competitor remained in Washington, stronger than ever with new money and new management. Since he couldn't buy the competition, Phil continued to try to beat it. He brought into the company a new production manager and a new advertising manager.

To add both ready money and prestige to *The Post*, he bought fifty-five per cent of the stock of a Washington radio station and the CBS affiliate, WTOP-TV. He bought a six-million-dollar building with facilities that could double the output of the previous plant, and he added color presses. At the dedication of the building, Secretary of Defense George Marshall said that *The Post* was "one of the most delicate instruments in America's arsenal of freedom." Kay's father furnished six million dollars to finance these additions and changes. The paper won the esteemed Sigma Delta Chi Award for distinguished journalism. In part of its new advertising campaign, it bragged that it printed more comics than in any other newspaper in America. (Later, they discovered that a paper in Pennsylvania actually had forty-two comic strips, two more than *The Post*.)

The newspaper became involved in the racial turmoil in Washington, where schools were segregated as were most other public facilities. Many "white" restaurants were closed to black people. This day-to-day racism was compounded by the government structure of the city. As prescribed by the Constitution, the city had no home rule. Instead, it was governed by a congressional committee. Since Congress was dominated by Southern legislators who had no interest in equal rights, black residents had no government representation.

Reporter Ben Bradlee wrote an article about a thirty-six hour period of violence that erupted when black residents tried to swim in municipal pools. Police using clubs studded with nails stopped the disturbance. Bradlee wanted this article printed on the front page. Phil knew that the story would embarrass the secretary of the interior, who was in charge of the pools. He made a bargain with the secretary to not print that story if the pools were opened to the black community.

Meanwhile, Kay accepted the customary female role of trying to make sure that everybody in the family was satisfied and happy. She eventually gave up her popular column. She explained, "After a while I got too busy with the family to keep it up, but I didn't dare tell Phil I was going to stop. I just stopped one day without telling him about it." Phil's mood-swings created a constant problem; Kay was unable to predict his behavior at any given time.

She developed a problem, too. She was continually tired, seeming always to need more sleep than she could get. At the end of the day, she was utterly exhausted just when Phil was eager to go out to dinner, off to entertainments, or on to meetings. Another serious problem for her revolved around entertaining at home. Agnes was famed as a hostess, and she set up a model for Kay that brought out her daughter's deep insecurities. On the other hand, Phil was used to lavish entertaining from his childhood days, and he scheduled many dinners and other get-togethers in his home with Kay as hostess.

The Post jumped into a conflict about communism. Many Americans, including some officials of the Department of State, believed that Soviet Premier Josef Stalin planned to incite a worldwide revolution for communism. This suspicion flared when Senator Joseph McCarthy charged that the Soviets had placed communist spies in U.S. government offices. McCarthy began holding hearings in the Senate, where government officials were often accussed of being communist, charges that were often based on little or no evidence. Over in the House of Representatives, the Committee on Un-American Activities, which included a newly elected Congressman Richard Nixon from California, also held hearing about government workers, writers, actors, and military officers.

The Post editorial pages declared that the committee had betrayed the most elementary rules of justice in its treatment of witnesses. The editorials went on to say that the conduct of the committee was dangerous, more un-American than that of any of the groups which

Ben Bradlee joined the *Washington Post* as a reporter. In later years, his editorship would help to make it one of the most respected newspapers in the world.

it was investigating. This criticism of what came to be known as the Red Scare was controversial. The *Times-Herald* attacked *The Post* position as un-American. Phil did not relent in his belief that too much time and money was spent on the hearings. He remained true to his often-stated belief that one goal of a newspaper was to further the acceptance of democracy and capitalism in this country. He said, "This is one newspaper's appeal to Americans to support action which will turn on the light of truth and restore the national harmony." In 1954, McCarthy was censured, officially criticized, by the Senate with a vote of 67 to 22. This move effectively ended the Senator's career.

Kay suffered a miscarriage that left her depressed in 1951. Still, she tried to become comfortable with her life as wife, mother, board member, house-keeper, and charity worker. She was busy with car-pools, birthday parties, sports lessons, and engagement-filled days. They bought a country home in Middleburg, Virginia, a retreat from the furor of Washington. Although Kay complained that packing up the children and household for weekends was a burden, the family enjoyed the trips to the home they called *Glen Welby*.

In a strong editorial endorsement, Phil supported General Dwight Eisenhower, a Republican, for president in 1952. This support caused family conflict. Eugene complained that Phil had not consulted him on this decision. Agnes scolded Phil for not being responsive to Eugene. From that time on, Phil was more careful to let Eugene in on his ideas and plans. Kay respected Phil for the way he related to Eugene.

In 1952, Kay gave birth to their fourth child, Stephen. Her mother sent a note saying she hoped that Kay's family would give her as much happiness as she (Kay) had given to Agnes' family. Agnes was working on her autobiography at that time. In her book, *Out of These Roots*, Agnes mentioned Kay only once, and that was to say that Kay sometimes attended parties at Mt. Kisco.

On the seventy-fifth anniversary of *The Washington Post*, Time called it the capital's "most independent and vigorous paper." Still, circulation had not reached the 200,000 mark, trailing both the *Star* and the *Times-Herald*.

That same year, Phil suddenly said that he was too ill to work. He asked other executives to take over for him. Most people, like Kay, assumed that he had simply worn himself out and would soon return to work after a good rest. He stayed home for three months, reading, playing with the new baby, and seeing some visitors.

Chapter Five

". . . good old mom, plodding along"

Kay asked her brother, Bill, a psychiatrist, to make an informal assessment of Phil's mental state. Bill said he was probably a manic-depressive, suffering from alternating extreme moods of excitement and depression. Phil was not interested in the diagnosis. He returned to work and once again was a cheerful and successful executive.

She was busy with Phil's schedule once he was back to work. He often wanted her to accompany him to social events. He liked to have her around when he was home, too. Phil liked to communicate, and Kay was a good listener. Phil had an amazing memory for conversations and incidents, and his re-telling of happenings at the office and at social events were good stories. They spent a lot of time together, with Kay often driving him to and from work and sometimes dozing on the sofa in his office when he worked late. Kay commented, "He got impatient if I talked too much so I sort of stopped talking."

Kay scheduled vacations when Phil could be with the children. One happy idea was to vacation in St. Petersburg, Florida, where they would watch the Yankees in spring training. Another vacation included going to a beach near Jacksonville, Florida, where they could also host an annual anniversary party for the paper's workers. Although they hired a caterer for the occasion, Kay found herself worrying and working with many arrangements.

Despite the vacations, Phil suffered from a number of illnesses and also began drinking more. As Agnes had done, Phil became more prone to depression, more abusive verbally, and less stable. Sometimes, Phil apologized to Kay after he had lost control due to alcohol. At these times, he said he would not drink to excess any more. When he was sober, Kay tried unsuccessfully to talk with him about his irrational and unpredictable behavior.

When they were getting along well, Phil and Kay talked a lot about the paper. In this way, Kay kept up with many of the new people, ideas, and changes in *The Post*. During these periods, he was exuberant and optimistic. At home he hunted, fished, and hiked with the children. He entertained them with stories and jokes. In public, he was the life of any party, and dynamic in the office. At other times, he was uncommunicative, uninterested, and vague. At home he was more and more critical of Kay—her clothes, the way she kept house, anything and everything.

In several ways, 1953 and 1954 were good years for *The Post*. Phil bought the remaining stock of WTOP. Now he had complete control of CBS radio and television outlets in Washington. Daily and Sunday circulation of passed two hundred thousand.

Phil took on new causes. He proposed an election financing bill to reduce the importance of contributions by special interest groups. His solution was to encourage private citizens to donate more to offset the special interests. Texas Senator Lyndon Johnson worked closely with Phil on this bill. The plan, called the Graham plan, resulted in the draft of a bill in the Senate signed by all but one senator. However, it failed to pass in the House. Phil and Senator Johnson remained good friends. The Grahams spent a weekend at the Johnson Texas ranch. There Kay felt uncomfortable because she believed that Johnson was using Phil for his prestige and power.

In January 1954, Eugene met with a representative of Colonel McCormick. The *Times-Herald* was up for sale due to McCormick's poor health and the fact that the paper was failing with falling circulation and annual losses of about half a million dollars a year. The two men agreed on a selling price of $8.5 million. On March 17, 1954, the deal was finalized. The paper became, temporarily *The Washington Post and Times-Herald*. When Eugene bought the paper, he said, "This makes *The Post* safe for Donny." The boy was then nine years old.

The two papers had served different audiences. The *Times Herald* had lots of features, columnists, sports, crime, and comics. *The Post* served more serious readers with more news-in-depth and more editorials. Phil's immediate job was to see that each audience was satisfied and that current and potential advertisers saw the value in the merger. Eugene printed a declaration of his policy including: "Editorially we shall continue our devotion to the cause of constitutional government, to the protection of civil liberties of every citizen, to home rule in Washington . . . and to international cooperation." Four months after the sale, the circulation for both daily and Sunday editions was just under four hundred thousand.

When Phil was optimistic and relaxed, Kay was also happy. The Virginia farm became a favorite retreat. They built a tennis court and two ponds. One pond was large enough for boating, and the family enjoyed a variety of boats from canoes and sailboats to a strong power boat for water skiing. They had many family meals together as well as lots of guests. Phil had fun with his children, organizing frog-catching expeditions, doing acrobatics, and making up games and riddles.

But this happiness did not last. In Phil's depressed periods, he felt increasingly uncomfortable about Eugene's financial help. He asserted that he could have made it on his own if he had not accepted Eugene's money. He warned Eugene not to interfere with the paper.

Kay also faced increasing problems that she acknowledged only vaguely. She was unhappy. She gained weight and paid little attention to how she dressed. Her mother seemed to her a competitor, not a friend or parent. Agnes usually spoke of her own achievements and showed no concern for Kay's life.

Kay believed that the only reason they had any friends was because of Phil's personality, not hers. Phil criticized her, calling her "Porky" for her weight gain. He even brought her a 'gift' from France—a sign from a butcher shop showing the head of a pig. He criticized her publicly as well as privately and, worst of all, in front of the children. Phil said he was embarrassed by his wife's looks and dress. He asked an editor at *Harper's Bazaar,* a fashion magazine, to help her, but this was not successful. Kay only became more shy.

Sometimes in self-defense, Kay laughed at Phil's jokes on her. "I was always the butt of family jokes. You know, good old Mom, plodding along. And I accepted it." She did everything she could to make Phil happy. She took charge of the children, managed the houses, and paid the bills. She sometimes apologized for the profanity he used in public.

To the outside world, Phil was the epitome of success. He was featured on the cover of *Time* magazine in April 1956 as an example of the American dream come true. The article called Phil ". . . an energetic charmer . . . (who) often has a senator, an ambassador, or a cabinet officer to his luncheon . . ." Their daughter Elizabeth, called Lally, admired her father for his exciting life and friends. She was much less interested in her mother, who seemed simply dull to her. Confused, Kay tried to win her daughter's appreciation by yielding to her every whim.

In the summer of 1957, Phil admitted that he was exhausted. He and Kay moved to Glen Welby, their country retreat in Virginia, to rest and enjoy the children. Kay spent most of her time with her husband. She said, "I would talk to him for eight hours at a time, trying to talk him out of the depression."

That same year, *The Post* was again involved in civil rights controversy. This time the situation arose when Arkansas Governor

Orval Faubus used the National Guard to keep nine black students out of Little Rock Central High, an all-white public school. Phil tried to encourage those involved to settle the matter without military intervention. But Eisenhower sent in federal troops to assure the safe passage of the black students, ending the immediate crisis. Phil believed this sending in the troops signaled the failure of the civil rights movement, and he mourned what he considered the end of a dream.

One night, Kay found Phil in extreme pain. He was unable to stop sobbing and was completely distraught about his inability to cope. A psychiatrist helped him through that particularly difficult period, but soon again he was going through a series of mood swings. Doctors ordered complete rest. He and Kay spent as much time as possible at Glen Welby with Kay ineffectively trying to talk him out of his illness. Then Phil returned to *The Post*, but it was obvious that he had not recovered. Part of his new and startling behavior was his frequent use of gutter language.

Less obvious was the fact that Phil suffered from overwhelming self-doubt, a desire to isolate himself, and indecision about even the smallest aspects of his life. He was completely dependent on Kay and insisted that she be there to listen to him at all times. Sometimes he visited his psychiatrist, sometimes read, and occasionally he played golf. He scarcely went to the office at all. The couple rarely entertained or went out, partly because Kay was afraid that Phil would drink too much. They sent out word that Phil needed a long rest on doctor's orders. Thanks to all the hard work he had put in during the last eleven years, the paper did quite well with Phil working from over the telephone.

From 1955-57, *The Post* had profits of over two million dollars a year. It became the nation's ninth largest newspaper, ranking seventh in advertising revenue in the country. Circulation was over 460,000 on Sundays and over 400,000 for dailies. The prices had risen